WISE WORDS

SHITTY BOOK

BY: CRISTOPHER WELCH

This is a shitty book that has wise words. If it has a purpose it is to be shitty. The book does have wise words though! These words are dedicated to all the people and things that make all the beauty in life possible. May this piece of work always be a light of life, love, and laughter across time.

WISE WORDS, SHITTY BOOK

DON'T SAY, JUST DO

SALMON, A GOOD FISH

THE TIME IS THERE

IT'S OKAY TO SAMPLE

DON'T WORRY ABOUT IT

BREATHE HOW YOU BREATHE

THERE WILL BE OPTIONS

LAUGH AND BE FRANK

POUR MORE
FOR MORE

ONLY CHANGE FOR YOURSELF

CLOCK IN, CLOCK OUT

THAT'S WHERE THINGS START

THOUGHTS ARE ALWAYS HAPPENING

TRUST RULES OVER ALL

REMEMBER; LIFE IS LOVE

EXPERIENCE NOT IN CONTROL

CONTINUE TO EMBRACE IMPERFECTIO NS

THESE MOMENTS ARE IMPORTANT

TOMORROW MAY NOT WORK

BEING WRONG, IT HAPPENS

DRINK WATER, FEEL GREAT

BE BOLD WITH PURPOSE

BUTTERFLIES DON'T LIKE CAGES

DESERVE HAPPINESS, EARN LOVE

BANANAS GO BAD QUICKLY

LUXURY, WHAT'S IT'S WORTH

PEOPLE ARE ACTUALLY PEOPLE

LOVE IS ALWAYS EVOLVING

JUST GO GET IT

THE MORNING SMELLS DIFFERENT

THINGS JUST COME OUT

EVEN A RIVER FALLS

TEARS BEAT LAUGHTER SOMETIMES

GOODBYE ALWAYS FOLLOWS HELLO

THAT'S HOW LIFE WORKS

BEST THE BEST YOU

DIFFERENT ISN'T ALWAYS BETTER

PREPARE TO SEE WHALES

LIFE'S A GREAT STORY

EVERY DECISION IS DESTINY

ENJOY PINEAPPLES ON SUNDAY

SMALL GOALS, BIG DREAMS

TIME IS AN ADVENTURE

THE EXPERIENCE IS EVERYTHING

WISE WORDS

SHITTY BOOK

www.ingramcontent.com/pod-product-compliance
Ingram Content Group UK Ltd.
Pitfield, Milton Keynes, MK11 3LW, UK
UKHW041632190726
13854UKWH00006B/2456